I0407431

TAMILNADU REPORTER

Dr.K.MURUGESAN,MBBS,AFIH

ISBN:1500174041
ISBN-13:9781500174040

Dr. K.MURUGESAN , MBBS,AFIH.,

DEDICATION

I Dedicate this book to the ancient kings and Kingdoms of Tamilnadu those who built many temples,cave Temples,forts and Dams in Tamilnadu which are now attract many tourists from all over the world .

TAMILNADU REPORTER

CONTENTS

Dr. K.MURUGESAN , MBBS,AFIH.,

TAMILNADU REPORTER

Dr. K.MURUGESAN , MBBS,AFIH.,

ACKNOWLEDGMENTS

This book is an effort to make a directory of general information about Tamilnadu to help people know the important places to visit for . The Tourist places listed in this book are for information purpose only . The list provided in this book is not a complete list .We will update missed places in our future editions to make this book a complete directory .

1. CHENNAI

Fort St. George Museum
Rajaji Salai, Fort St George, Chennai, Tamil Nadu 600009

Marina beach
Marina Beach Road, Chennai

Santhome Church
38, Santhome High Road, Chennai, Tamil Nadu 600004

Dr. K.MURUGESAN , MBBS,AFIH.,

Gandhi Mandapam
Sardar Patel Rd, Guindy National Park, Guindy, Chennai, Tamil Nadu 600022

Rajaji Memorial
Guindy National Park, Guindy, Chennai, Tamil Nadu 600022

Kamaraj Memorial
Guindy National Park, Guindy, Chennai, Tamil Nadu 600022

Bhaktavatsalam Memorial
Guindy National Park, Guindy, Chennai, Tamil Nadu 600022

Vivekanandar Illam
Marina Beach Road, Neelam Basha Dargapuram, Kamarajar salai, Triplicane, Chennai, Tamil Nadu 600005

TAMILNADU REPORTER

Kolavai Lake
Kolavai Lake, Tamil Nadu 603002

Located at 500 meters near Old Chengelpet bus terminus .

Pulicat or Pazhaverkadu
important places to visit here are Pulicat Lake and Old Dutch Cemetary

Mamallapuram
Located at 60km from Chennai .it is known for its stone temples built by Pallava Dynasty in the 7th and 8th Centuries .

Vedanthangal Bird Sanctuary
Located in Madhuranthagam Taluk of kanchipuram district . various Birds from all over the world visit this Sanctuary in each Year.

Kapaleeshwarar Temple
Kapaleesvarar Sannadhi Street, Vinayaka Nagar Colony, Mylapore, Chennai, Tamil Nadu 600004

Dr. K.MURUGESAN , MBBS,AFIH.,

Island Grounds
Anna Salai Mount Road, The Island, Park
Town, Chennai, Tamil Nadu 600003

Madras High Court
High Ct Rd, Parry's Corner, George Town,
Chennai, Tamil Nadu 600108

International Theosophical Society
Blavatsky Avenue
600020 Adyar , TN
India

Adyar Banyan Tree
Schwarz Ave, Theosophical Society, Besant
Nagar, Chennai, Tamil Nadu 600090

Annai Vailankanni Shrine
Besant Nagar,
Chennai – 600 090

Ashtalakshmi Temple
Elliots beach, Besant Nagar, Chennai, Tamil
Nadu 600090

Kalakshetra Foundation
Kalakshetra Rd, Radhakrishnan Nagar,
Thiruvanmiyur, Chennai, Tamil Nadu 600041

TAMILNADU REPORTER

Birla Planetarium
Gandhi Mandapam Rd, Duraisamy Nagar,
Kotturpuram, Chennai, Tamil Nadu 600025
Phone: 044 2441 0025

Periyar Science and Technology Centre
No., 6, Gandhi Mandapam Rd, Surya Nagar,
Kotturpuram, Chennai, Tamil Nadu 600085

St. Thomas Mount
Parangi Malai, St Thomas Mount, Ramapuram,
Tamil Nadu 600016

Ripon Building
Address: Sydenhams Rd, Kannappar Thidal,
Periyamet, Chennai, Tamil Nadu 600003

Government Museum
Address: Beside Government Maternity
Hospital, Pantheon Road, Egmore, Chennai,
Tamil Nadu 600008

Dr. K.MURUGESAN , MBBS,AFIH.,

National Art Gallery
Address: Government museum, Pantheon Rd,
Egmore, Chennai, Tamil Nadu 600008

Connemara Public Library
Address: Museum Compound, Pantheon Road,
Egmore, Chennai, Tamil Nadu 600008

Valluvar Kottam
Tirumurthy Nagar, Nungambakkam, Chennai,
Tamil Nadu 600034

Guindy National Park
Rangeguindy, Opp IIT Madras, Chennai, Tamil
Nadu-600025

Children's Park
Sardar Patel Road , Guindy, Chennai 600032,
India

TAMILNADU REPORTER

Guindy Snake Park
Sardar Patel Road ,Nr. Guindy National Park, Chennai, India

Arignar Anna Zoological Park
GST Road, Vandalur, Chennai, Tamil Nadu 600048

Chokhi Dhani
NH-4, Near Queensland Theme Park, Kevlur Road Tandalam Sriperumbudur, Chennai, Tamil Nadu 602105

Arulmigu Thiyagarajaswamy Temple
Address: Sannathi Street, TS Gopal Nagar, Tiruvottiyur, Chennai, Tamil Nadu 600019

Thiruverkadu Devi Karumariamman Temple
Sannathi Street, Vallikollaimedu, Thiruverkadu, Chennai, Tamil Nadu 600077

2 . THIRUVALLUR

Thiruthani Murugan Temple
Address: Thiruthani Hill, Thiruthani, Tamil
Nadu 631209
Phone: 044 2788 5243

Sri Kothandaramaswamy Temple
Address: Sannathi Street, SH 63, Tamil Nadu
614019

Queens Land
Address: Chennai-Bengaluru Highway,
Palanjur, Sembarambakkam, Chennai, Tamil
Nadu 600123

Arulmigu Vaidhya Veeraraghava Swamy Temple
Address: Adjacent to Temple Tank, Sannadhi
St, Tiruvallur, Tamil Nadu 602001

TAMILNADU REPORTER

Sri Vadaranyeswarar Temple
Address: Thiruvalangadu Road, District
Tiruvallur, Thiruvalangadu, Tamil Nadu 631210

Sri Ranganatha Perumal
Address: Devadhanam to Thachur cross road,
6Kms Anna nagar to Thanchur Cross Road -
18Kms, via Ponneri, Tiruvallur, Tamil Nadu
601203

Om Sri Bhavani Amman Temple
Periyapalayam,
Tiruvallore District,
Tamil Nadu.
India

Sri Theertheswarar Swami Devasthanam
Address: 91, West Tank Street, Tiruvallur, Tamil
Nadu 602001

Poondi Reservoir
Poondi Lake, Tiruvallur, Tamil Nadu

Dr. K.MURUGESAN , MBBS,AFIH.,

3.KANCHIPURAM

Kamakshi Amman Temple
Address: New No. 6, Old No. 144/A, Kamakshi Amman, Sannathi St, Periya, Kanchipuram, Tamil Nadu 631502

Varadharaja Perumal Temple
Address: Nethaji Nagar, Kanchipuram, Tamil Nadu 631501

Kanchi Kailasanathar Temple
Address: Pillaiyarpalayam, Kanchipuram, Tamil Nadu 631501

TAMILNADU REPORTER

Devaraja swami temple
Address: Chithathur, Tamil Nadu 604410

Thiru Ekambaranathar Temple
Address: Sannathi Street, Near Railway Station,
Periya, Kanchipuram, Tamil Nadu 631502
Phone: 044 2722 2084

Kanchi Kudil
Address: 53 A, SVN Pillai Street, Kanchipuram,
Tamil Nadu 631502
Phone: 044 2722 7680

Sri Kachabeswarar Temple
Address: Nellukara St, Periya, Kanchipuram,
Tamil Nadu 631502
Phone: 044 2723 3384

Vaikunta Perumal Temple
Address: Vaigundaperumal Koil St, Periya,
Kanchipuram, Tamil Nadu 631502

Dr. K.MURUGESAN , MBBS,AFIH.,

Kanchi Kamakoti Peetham
Address: 1, Salai St, Periya, Kanchipuram, Tamil
Nadu 631502
Phone: 044 2722 2115

Ulagalantha Perumal Temple
Address: Kamakshi Amman Sannidhi Street,
Periya, Kanchipuram, Tamil Nadu 631502

Jain Temple
Address: Ennaikara St, Ennaikaran,
Kanchipuram, Tamil Nadu 631501

Sri Prasanna Venkatesa Perumal Temple
Address: Mutthialpettai, Kanchipuram, Tamil
Nadu 631601

Arulmigu Vijayaraghava Perumal
Thirukovil
Address: Thiruppukuzhi, Tamil Nadu 631551
Phone: 044 2724 6501

TAMILNADU REPORTER

Chitragupta temple
Address: Hospital Rd, Nellukara st,
Kanchipuram, Tamil Nadu 631501

Eri Katha Ramar Temple
Address: Madurantakam, Tamil Nadu 603306

Sri Pandu Ranga Perumal Temple
Address: Thennangur, Tamil Nadu 604408

4.VELLORE

Vellore Fort
Address: Balaji Nagar, Vellore, Tamil Nadu
632004

Muthu Mandapam
opposite to New Bustand, New Bridge Rd,
Vevekanandar Nagar, Thottapalayam, Vellore,
Tamil Nadu 632012

Jalakandeswarar Temple
Address: Balaji Nagar, Vellore, Tamil Nadu
632004

State Government Museum
Address: Balaji Nagar, Vellore, Tamil Nadu
632004

TAMILNADU REPORTER

CMC Hospital
Address: Arcot Rd, Thottapalayam, Vellore, Tamil Nadu 632004

Shri Margabandeeswarar Temple
Address: Virinjipuram, Tamil Nadu 632104

Sri Renugambal Temple
Address: Off Thiruvannamalai to, Polur - Vellore Road, A.K, Padavedu Temple Rd, Padavedu, Tamil Nadu 606905
Phone: 04181 248 224

Amirthi Zoological Park
Address: Kannamangalam, Kathalampattu R.F, Amirthi, Vellore, Tamil Nadu 632102

Thiruvalam Shiva Temple
Address: Thiruvalam, Tamil Nadu 632515

Mordhana dam
Jangalapalli R.F.,
Tamil Nadu 632601

Dr. K.MURUGESAN , MBBS,AFIH.,

5.THIRUVANNAMALAI

Arunachalesvara Temple
Address: Pavazhakundur, Tiruvannamalai,
Tamil Nadu 606601

Sri Ramana Ashram
Address: Chengam Road, National Highway
66,, Thamarai Nagar, Tiruvannamalai, Tamil
Nadu 606603
Phone: 04175 237 200

Sathanur Dam
Ponnaiyur R.F., Tamil Nadu 606706

TAMILNADU REPORTER

Sri Renugambal Temple
Address: Off Thiruvannamalai to, Polur - Vellore Road, A.K, Padavedu Temple Rd, Padavedu, Tamil Nadu 606905
Phone: 04181 248 224

Javadhu Hills
Jamunamarathur, Tiruvannamalai 635703

Kubera Lingam
Kubera Nagar, Vengikkal, Tiruvannamalai, Tamil Nadu 606604

Sri Seshadri Swamigal Ashramam
Address: National Highway 66, Thamarai Nagar, Tiruvannamalai, Tamil Nadu 606601
Phone: 04175 236 999

Dr. K.MURUGESAN , MBBS,AFIH.,

Arcot lutheran Church
Address: SH 9, Mathalangulam,
Tiruvannamalai, Tamil Nadu 606601

Sri Durgai Amman Temple
Tiruvennanallur, Tiruvannamalai,
Tamil Nadu, 606601

Melmalai Kubera Perumal Temple
Address: Kubera Nagar, Vengikkal,
Tiruvannamalai, Tamil Nadu 606604

6.KRISHNAGIRI

Krishnagiri Dam
Krishnagiri Dam, Tamil Nadu 635101

Kelavarapalli Dam
Address: Bridge Rd, Tamil Nadu 635109

Pambar Dam
Address: Uthangarai, Tamil Nadu 635207

Thally (Little England)
Denkanikottai Taluk,
Krishnagiri district

Sri Chandra Choodeswara Temple
Address: Sanasandiram, Hosur, Tamil Nadu 635109

7.DHARMAPURI

Hogenakkal Falls
Address: Dharmapuri-Hogenakkal Road, Dist,
Hogenakkal, Tamil Nadu 636810

Theerthamalai Temple
Address: 4th Cross, Palepalle, Tamil Nadu
635120

Shri Theerthagirishwarar Temple
Address: Kuppusamy Naidu St, Dharmapuri,
Tamil Nadu 636701

Siva Subramania Swamy Temple

TAMILNADU REPORTER

Address: Dharmapuri, Tamil Nadu 636701

Chenraya Perumal Temple
Address: Adhiyaman Kottai, A.Jettihalli, Tamil Nadu 636807

Mt. Carmel Church
Address: Pallipatti, Tamil Nadu 635301

Crocodile Park
Address: Hogenakkal-Anchetty Rd, Hogenakkal, Tamil Nadu 636810

Dr. K.MURUGESAN , MBBS,AFIH.,

8.VILUPPURAM

Gingee Fort
Address: NH 66, Gingee, Tamil Nadu 604202

Thiruvamathur Shiva Temple
Address: Thiruvamathur, Tamil Nadu 605402
Phone: 04146 223 379

Sri Angala Parameswari Temple
Address: Melmalaiyanur, Kodukankuppam,
Tamil Nadu 604204
Phone: 04145 234 229

TAMILNADU REPORTER

St Antony's Church
Address: Melnariyappanur, Tamil Nadu 606201

Ulagalantha Perumal Temple
Address: Tirukoilur-Asanur Road, Thirukovilur, Tamil Nadu 605757

Kalvarayan Hill
Ezhuthur, Tamil Nadu 606207

Marakkanam Beach
Address: Kaipenikuppam, Tamil Nadu 604303

Sadhana Forest
Address: 1, Sadhana Forest Road, Auroville, Tamil Nadu 605101
Phone: 0413 267 7682

Sri Mailam Murugan Temple
Address: Adheenakarther, SSBS Thirumadam, Mailam, Tamil Nadu 604304
Phone: 04147 241 223

Anjaneyar Temple
Address: Thiru Vi Ka Street, Villupuram, Tamil

Dr. K.MURUGESAN , MBBS,AFIH.,

Nadu 605602

Svaram Musical Instruments and Research
Kottakarai, Irumbai B.O
Auroville 605111
Tamil Nadu

Arulmigu Lakshmi Narashima Swamy Temple
Address: Villupuram, Parikkal, Tamil Nadu 607204

Irumbai Shri Maha Kaleshwar Siva Temple
Address: Irumbai,Auroville, Tamil Nadu 605111

Sri Raghuttama Swamy Moola Brindavana Uttaradimath
Manmpoondi ,Tirukoilur ,
Villupuram,Tamilnadu 605759

Sri Valeeswarar Temple
Address: Koliyanur, Tamil Nadu 605103

9.CADDALORE

Nataraja Temple
Address: Chidambaram, Tamil Nadu 608001

Pichavaram Mangrove forest
Pichavaram , Chidambaram ,Cuddalore District

Peaceful Dam
Address: Kattumannarkoil, Tamil Nadu 608701

Velliyangal Dam
Address: Lalpettai, Tamil Nadu 608701

Lalpet Veraanam View Point
Address: Lalpettai, Tamil Nadu 608303

periyandavar temple
Perperiyankuppm Road, Panruti, Tamil Nadu

Dr. K.MURUGESAN , MBBS,AFIH.,

Dhanvantri Temple
Tagore St Panruti, Tamil Nadu 607106

Silver Beach
Cuddalore

Fort St. David
Address: Devanampattinam, Cuddalore, Tamil Nadu 607001

Pataleeswarar Temple
Address: Car Street, Muthaiya Nagar, Thirupapuliyur, Cuddalore, Tamil Nadu 607002

Vriddhagiriswarar Temple
Vriddhachalam, Cuddalore district

Devanathaswamy temple
Address: Thiruvandipuram, Tamil Nadu 607401

Veeranam Lake
kattumannarkoil, Cuddalore district, Tamil Nadu

10.SALEM

Mettur Dam
Mettur, Salem District, Tamil Nadu

Shevaroy Temple
Address: Yercaud, Yercaud, Tamil Nadu 636602

Yercaud Lake
Yercaud, Tamil Nadu 636601

Anna Park
Address: 30/68, Ondikadai, Salem - Yercaud
Ghat Road, Yercaud, Tamil Nadu 636601

Dr. K.MURUGESAN , MBBS,AFIH.,

Kiliyur Falls
Address: Killiyur Road, Pattipadi, Tamil Nadu 636601

Lady's Seat
Address: Yercaud, Tamil Nadu 636601

Gents Seat
Address: Near T.V.Station, Ladies Seat Rd, Yercaud, Tamil Nadu 636601

Kurumbapatti Zoological Park
Address: Kurumbampatti, Tamil Nadu 636008

Manjakuttai View Point
Address: Yercaud, Tamil Nadu 636602

Botanical Garden
Address: 30/68, Ondikadai, Salem - Yercaud Ghat Road, Yercaud, Tamil Nadu 636601

TAMILNADU REPORTER

Linga Bhairavi Temple
Address: College Road Omalur
Saminaikanpatti Linga Bhairavi Valagam,
Salem, Tamil Nadu 636011

Kanjamalai
14 km west of Salem District

Karadiyoor View Point
Address: Nagloor Kolakoor Road, Karadiyoor,
Elavadi, Tamil Nadu 636602

Arulmigu Sugavaneswarar Swamy Temple
Address: First Agraharam, Salem, Tamil Nadu
636001

Paravasa Ulagam
Address: Salem to Namakkal Highway, NH-7,
KK Valasu, Mallur, Salem, Tamil Nadu 636203

Children's Seat
Address: Yercaud, Tamil Nadu 636601

Dr. K.MURUGESAN , MBBS,AFIH.,

Yercaud Rose Garden
Address: Yercaud, Tamil Nadu 636601

Deer Park
Address: Lady's seat road, Yercaud, Tamil Nadu 636601

Yercaud Lake Boat House
Address: 30/68, Ondikadai, Salem - Yercaud Ghat Road, Yercaud, Tamil Nadu 636601

Sri Kailasanathar Temple
Address: Tharamangalam, Tamil Nadu 636502

Mettur Park
Address: Unnamed Road, Mettur, Tamil Nadu 636401

1008 Shiva Temple
Address: Srinagar - Kanyakumari Hwy, Ariyanur, Salem, Tamil Nadu 636308

TAMILNADU REPORTER

Silk World
Address: Yercaud, Tamil Nadu 636601

Raja Rajeshwari Temple
Address: Yercaud, Tamil Nadu 636601

Siddhar Kovil
Address: Siddhar Kovil Rd, Kanjamalai R.F.,
Tamil Nadu 636307

Sacred Heart Church
Address: Hill Church Road, Yercaud, Tamil
Nadu 636601

Anaimaduvu Reservoir
Address: Valappadi, Tamil Nadu 636139

Thanthondreeswarar Temple
Address: Ayothiyapattinam - Belur - Kilakkadu
Rd, Belur, Tamil Nadu 636104

Dr. K.MURUGESAN , MBBS,AFIH.,

Tipperary View Point
Address: Tipperary Road,, Tipperary Estate, Yercaud, Tamil Nadu 636601

Kallaru Falls
Address: Manjavadi R.F., Tamil Nadu 636601

Hairpin Bends to Yercaud
Address: State Highway 188, Yercaud, Tamil Nadu 636601

Skandasramam Murugan Temple
Address: Udayapatti, Salem, Tamil Nadu 636140

Pagoda View Point
Address: Pagoda Point Road, Yercaud, Tamil Nadu 636601

Gowri Woodlands Estate Lake
Address: Yercaud, Tamil Nadu 636602

TAMILNADU REPORTER

Kottai Mariamman Temple
Address: Fairlands Main Rd, First Agraharam,
Salem, Tamil Nadu 636001

Linga Bhairavi Temple
Mahadevi Trust, Linga Bhairavi Valagam,
Saminaikanpatti ,Omalur tk, Salem 636011

Bathrakaliamman Temple
Mecheri, Salem 636451

Sankagiri Fort
Sankagiri Hills , Sankari Taluka, Salem 637301

Sri Ramar Temple
Athur Vriddachalam Highway, Salem

Poiman Karadu
Salem- Namakkal National Highway ,9 Km
From Salem, Salem

11.NAMAKKAL

Anjaneya Temple
Address: Hanumar Koil Street, Thillaipuram,
Namakkal, Tamil Nadu 637001
Phone: 04286 233 999

Narasimhaswamy Temple
Address: Arulmigu Narasimha Swamy Temple,
Namakkal, Tamil Nadu 637001
Phone: 04286 233 999

Seeku Parai View Point
Address: Kolli Hills, District, Semmedu, Tamil
Nadu

Ettukai Amman Temple
Address: MDR690, Ariyurnadu, Tamil Nadu
637411

TAMILNADU REPORTER

Siddhar Caves
Kolli Hills, Namakkal

Thathagiri Murugan Temple
Address: Akkiyampatti, Tamil Nadu 637409

Kolli Hill Forest
Address: Sangarai - Navagadu, Edappulinadu,
Tamil Nadu 637411

Agaya Gangai Water falls
Kolli hills,
Namakkal

Arapaleeshwar Temple
Karavallicombai, 637411

Boating Point - Kolli Hills
Address: Jambuthu R.F., Tamil Nadu 637411

Dr. K.MURUGESAN , MBBS,AFIH.,

Kolli Hills Resorts
Address: Boat House Road, Opp Govt
Horticulture Farm, Semmedu PO, Kolli Hills Tk,
Namakkal, Tamil Nadu 641114

Botanical Garden
Address: Jambuthu R.F., Tamil Nadu 637411

Valappurnadu View Point
Address: Valappurnadu, kolli Hills,Tamil Nadu
637411

Namakkal Fort
Address: Salem - Namakkal - Trichy Rd,
Thillaipuram, Namakkal, Tamil Nadu 637001

Maasila Falls
Address: Ariyurnadu, Tamil Nadu 637411

Jedarpalayam Dam Park
Address: Jedarpalayam Road, Mariyamman
Padugai, Tamil Nadu 637213

12.ERODE

Magudeswarar alayam
Address: Kodumudi, Tamil Nadu 638151

Sri Sangameshwarar Temple
Address: Bhavani, Tamil Nadu 638301
Phone: 04256 230 192

Kodiveri Dam
Periyakodiveri, Tamil Nadu 638503

Bannari Amman Temple
Address: National Highway 209,
Sathyamangalam Taluk, Erode District,
Bannari, Tamil Nadu 638401
Phone: 04295 243 289

Dr. K.MURUGESAN , MBBS,AFIH.,

Dheeran Chinnamalai Mani Mandapam
Jayavilas Niwas, Pirivu Road, Sankari RS - Erode
Privu Rd, Sankari, Tamil Nadu 637303

Kalingarayan Anicut
Address: Kalingarayanpalayam, Bhavani, Tamil
Nadu 638316

Odapalli Barrage Park
Address: Erode-Kokkarayanpettai Rd,
Pallipalayam, Tamil Nadu 638007

VOC Park
Address: Thirunagar Colony, Erode, Tamil
Nadu 638001

Thanthai Periyar Memorial House
Address: Marapalam, Erode, Tamil Nadu
638001

Government Museum
Address: VOC Park Approach Road, Thirunagar
Colony, Erode, Tamil Nadu 638001

TAMILNADU REPORTER

Periya Maariyamman Temple
Address: Arulmigu Periyamariamman temple, Brough Rd, Chidambaram Colony, Erode, Tamil Nadu 638001

Bhavanisagar Water Reservoir and Dam
Address: Bhavanisagar, Tamil Nadu 638451

Jedarpalayam Dam Park
Address: Jedarpalayam Road, Mariyamman Padugai, Tamil Nadu 637213

Chennimalai Murugan Temple
Address: Chennimalai, Tamil Nadu 638051

Sathyamangalam Tiger Reserve
Address: Talamalai R.F., Tamil Nadu

Vellode Bird Sanctuary
Address: Vadamugam Vellode, Tamil Nadu 638112

Dr. K.MURUGESAN , MBBS,AFIH.,

Sri Kongalamman Temple
Nethaji Road,Thirunagar Colony, Erode

Arulmigu Arudra Kabaleswarar Temple
Address: Eswaran Kovil Street, Erode Fort,
Erode, Tamil Nadu 638001

Cauvery River
Erode

CSI Brough Memorial Church
Address: Brough Rd, CSI Institutions Campus,
Chidambaram Colony, Erode, Tamil Nadu
638001

Nattatreswaran Temple
Kaveri River, via Erode-Karur Rd/Karur Rd,
Erode 637210

Masjid Mahmoodia
Address: Thirunagar Colony, Erode, Tamil
Nadu 638003

13.NILGIRIS

Upper Bhavani Lake
Snowdown Road Ooty Commercial Roadd
Ooty, Garden Road Ooty, Ooty 643001

Kodanad View Point
Kodanadu , Nilgiris, Kotagiri

Nilgiri Mountain Railway
Ooty

Pykara Lake
Ooty

Heritage Train
Coonoor

Dr. K.MURUGESAN , MBBS,AFIH.,

Avalanche Lake
Avalance, Ooty

Emerald Lake
Emerald Village .Nilgiris, Ooty

Murugan Temple
Elk Hill, Ooty 643001

Dolphin's Nose
Coonoor Centre, Coonoor 643101

14.ARIYALUR

Sri Bragadeeswarar Temple
Gangaikonda Chola Puram,
Ariyalur district

Karaivetti Bird Sanctuary
Address:
Ariyalur district
Tamil Nadu 621653

Melapalur Siva Temple
Address: 6/154, Sivan Kovil St, Melapalur,
Ariyalur, Tamil Nadu 621707

Sri Draupathi Amman Temple
Address: Trichy Main Rd, Melapalur, Tamil
Nadu 621707

Dr. K.MURUGESAN , MBBS,AFIH.,

Sri Kamba Perumal Temple
Address: Melapalur, Tamil Nadu 621707

Vartharaja Perumal Temple
Address: Melapalur, Tamil Nadu 621707

Sri Maha Kaliyamman Temple
Address: Melapalur, Tamil Nadu 621707

Arulmigu Sri Angala Parameswari Amman Temple
Address: 6/154, Sivan Kovil St, Melapalur, Sivan Kovil St, Melapalur, Ariyalur, Tamil Nadu 621707

Meenatchi Sundareswarar Koil
Melapalur

Keezhaiyur Twin Temple
Keezhaiyur

Thirumazhapadi Shiva Temple
Address: Thirumazhapadi, Tamil Nadu 621851

Nanthiyemperumal Temple
Address: Thirumalapadi Rd, Thirumazhapadi,
Tamil Nadu 621851

Karkodeswarar
Address: Kamarasavalli,Ariyalur, Tamil Nadu
621715

Buddha Statues
Vikkiramangalam
Ariyalur
Tamil Nadu 621701

Shivan Kovil
Address: Sendurai, Tamil Nadu 621714

Sennivanam Shivan Temple
Address: Sennivanam, Tamil Nadu 621718

Vanniamman Anandavalliamman Temple
Address: Arangottai, Sripurandan North, Tamil
Nadu 6217

Kodandaramaswamy Temple
Ariyalur

Elakurichi Adaikala Madha Shrine
Address: Elakurichi, Ariyalur, Thirumanur,
Tamil Nadu 621715

15.PERAMBALUR

Ranjankudi Fort
Address: Perambalur, Tamil Nadu 621115

National Fossil Wood Park
Address: Madha Kovil Street, Thiruvakkarai,
Tamil Nadu 605501

Siruvachur Sri Madhurakaliamman Temple
Address: Siruvachur, Tamil Nadu 621113

Koraiyar Falls
Thondamanthurai
Perambalur distric

Thandayuthapani Temples
Address: Chettikulam, Tamil Nadu 621104

Mayil Ootru Waterfalls
Address: Melapuliyur,Tamil Nadu 621101

16.THIRUCHIRAPALLI

Kallanai
Tamil Nadu 620013

Mukkombu Upper Dam
Address: NH 67, Tamil Nadu 639115

Rani Mangammal District Museum
Address: Singarathope, Devathanam,
Tiruchirappalli, Tamil Nadu 620002

Sri Ranganatha Swamy Temple
Address: Srirangam, Tiruchirappalli, Tamil
Nadu 620006

Tiruchirapalli Rock Fort
Teppakulam, Tiruchirappalli, Tamil Nadu
620002

Ucchi Pillayar Temple
Address: Tiruchirapalli Rock Fort, N Andar St,
Teppakulam, Tiruchirappalli, Tamil Nadu

Dr. K.MURUGESAN , MBBS,AFIH.,

620002

Thayumanaswami Temple
Address: Rockfort complex, South Street, Teppakulam, Tiruchirappalli, Tamil Nadu 620002

Jambukeswarar Temple
Address: N Car St, Thiruvanaikoil, Srirangam, Tiruchirappalli, Tamil Nadu 620005

Samayapuram Mariamman Temple
Address: 13/1, Maruthur Rd, Tiruchirappalli, Maruthur Rd, Tiruchirappalli, Tamil Nadu 621112

Vekkali Amman Temple
Address: Vekkaliyamman, S S Kovil Street, Woraiyur, Tiruchirappalli, Tamil Nadu 620003

Butterfly Park
Address: Tropical Butterfly Conservatory Campus, Srirangam Taluk, Tiruchirappalli District, Melur, Tamil Nadu 620006

Vayalur Murugan Temple
Address: Vayalur, Tiruchirappalli, Tamil Nadu 620021

TAMILNADU REPORTER

Srirangam Island
Tiruchirappalli

Sri Pundarikaksha Perumal Temple
Address: Sannathi steert, Thillampatti,
Agraharam, Thiruvellarai, Tamil Nadu 621009

Our Lady of Lourdes Church
Address: College Rd, Annamalai Nagar,
Teppakulam, Tiruchirappalli, Tamil Nadu
620002

Erumbeeswarar Temple
Address: Malaikoil, Thiruverumbur, Tamil Nadu
620013

Shri Ayyappan Temple
Address: No-2, Lawsons Rd, Cantonment,
Tiruchirappalli, Tamil Nadu 620001

Sri Gneeliwaneswarar Temple
Address: Thiruppainjeeli, Tamil Nadu 621005

Arulmigu Uthamar Kovil
Address: Trichy-Salem Main Road
Manachanallur, Taluk, Tiruchirappalli, Tamil
Nadu 621216

Dr. K.MURUGESAN , MBBS,AFIH.,

World War I Memorial
Address: Nagapattinam - Coimbatore - Gundlupet Hwy, Palakarai, Tharanallur, Tiruchirappalli, Tamil Nadu 620008

Anna Science Center
Address: Near karupu swamy kovil, Vadakkadu - Alangudi Road, Tiruchirappalli, Tamil Nadu 620007

Manicka Vinayagar Temple
Address: Teppakulam, Tiruchirappalli, Tamil Nadu 620002

Arulmigu Boominathar Temple
Address: L.F. Road, Mannachanallur, Tiruchirappalli, Tamil Nadu 621005

Varahi Amman Temple
Address: Kulumani Main Rd, Mangala Nagar, Woraiyur, Tiruchirappalli, Tamil Nadu 620120

Kattu Azhagiya Singa Perumal Temple
Address: Srirangam, Tiruchirappalli, Tamil Nadu 620005

TAMILNADU REPORTER

Divya Desam Kamalavalli Nachiyar Kovil
Address: 25, Nachiyar kovil Sannathi St,
Woraiyur, Tiruchirappalli, Tamil Nadu 620017

Tiruppaatrurai Adhimooleswarar Temple
Address: Road Tirupalathurai, Panayapuram,
Tamil Nadu 620005

Amma Mandapam
Address: Srirangam, Tiruchirappalli, Tamil
Nadu 620008

Uyyakondan Thirumalai Temple
Address: No-203, Vayalur Rd, MM Nagar,
Tiruchirappalli, Tamil Nadu 620102

Aayiram Kaal Mandapam
Address: Srirangam Temple Elephant Shelter, E
Uthrai St, Sriramapuram, Srirangam,
Tiruchirappalli, Tamil Nadu 620006

Subramaniya Swamy Temple
Address: Vayalur Murugan Temple Road,
Gramam Vayalur, Tiruchirappalli, Tamil Nadu
620102

Dr. K.MURUGESAN , MBBS,AFIH.,

Gandhi Childrens Park
Address: Butterworth Rd, Teppakulam,
Tiruchirappalli, Tamil Nadu 620002

Shri Panjavarna Swamy Kovil
Address: 44-a, Panchavarna Swami Temple
Street, Woraiyur, Tiruchirappalli, Tamil Nadu
620003

Sri Lakshmi Narasimha Perumal Temple
Address: Perumal Kovil St, Allithurai,
Tiruchirappalli, Tamil Nadu 620102

St. Joseph's church
Address: 15, 5th Main Rd 2nd Cross, Srinivasa
Nagar South, Srinivasa Nagar North, Srinivasa
Nagar, Tiruchirappalli, Tamil Nadu 620017

17.KARUR

Pasupathieswarer Temple
National Highway 7, Karur 639001

Sadasiva Brahmendra Samadhi
Nerur, Karur

Kalyana Venkattaramasami Temple
Thanthoni , Karur

Pugazhimalai Shree Arupadai Murugan Temple
Atop Hillock, Pugalur, Karur

Aathupalayam Dam
Karvazhi Village, K.Paramathi Taluk, Karur

Dr. K.MURUGESAN , MBBS,AFIH.,

18.THIRUPPUR

Avinashi Temple
Avinashi Town, Tiruppur

Thirumoorthi Dam
Udumalpet, Tiruppur

Amaravathi Crocodile Farm
Amaravathi, Tiruppur

Arulmigu Kadu Anumantharaya Swamy Temple
Dharapuram, Tiruppur

Noyyal River
Vellingiri Hills, Western Ghats, Tiruppur

19.COIMBATORE

Kovai Kutrallam
Kovai Kutralam Road
Booluvampatti, Tamil Nadu 641114

Poondi Velliangiri Thirukovil Adivaram
Address: Coimbatore, Tamil Nadu 641114

G.D.Naidu Industrial Exhibition
734, President Hall, Avinashi Road, Anna Salai,
Coimbatore – 641018

Marudhamalai
Address: Temple Rd, Maruthamalai,
Coimbatore, Tamil Nadu 641046

Dr. K.MURUGESAN , MBBS,AFIH.,

Karamadai Ranganathar Temple
Address: Coimbatore - Mettupalayam Road, Karamadai, Tamil Nadu 641104

Palani Murugan temple
Address: Giri Veethi, Palani, Tamil Nadu 624601

Anamalai Tiger Reserve
Address: Pollachi, Tamil Nadu 642101

Solaiyar Dam
Address: Valparai, Tamil Nadu 642125

Monkey Falls
Address: Coimbatore, Tamil Nadu 642101

20.NAGAPATTINAM

Kayarohanaswami Temple
Address: Neela Sannathi, ASN Colony, Melakottaivasal, Nagapattinam, Tamil Nadu 611003

Nagore Dargah Masjid
Address: New Bazzar Line, Nagore, Nagapattinam, Tamil Nadu 611002

Basilica of Our Lady of Good Health
Address: Velankanni, Nagapattinam, Tamil Nadu 611111

Brahmapureeswarar Temple
Thirukkuvalai
Nagapattinam district

21.TANJAVUR

Brihadisvara Temple
Address: Membalam Rd, Balaganapathy Nagar, Thanjavur, Tamil Nadu 613007

Royal Palace Museum
Address: Rajakrisnapuram, Thanjavur, Tamil Nadu 613001

Saraswathi Mahal Library
Address: E Main St, Rajakrisnapuram, Thanjavur, Tamil Nadu 613001

Tamil University
Address: Tamil University Road, Thanjavur, Tamil Nadu 613010

Brahma Sira Kandeeswarar Temple
Thirukkandiyur, Thanjavur

TAMILNADU REPORTER

Aiyarappar temple
Address: SH 22, Thiruvaiyaru, Tamil Nadu
613204

Agniswarar Temple
Address: Aduthurai-Kuthalam Road,
Kanjanoor, Tamil Nadu 609804

Raaghu Sthalam
Thirunageswaram, Kumbakonam 612204

Thirunallar Saneeshwara Bhagavan Temple
Thirunallar,
Tanjavur

Dr. K.MURUGESAN , MBBS,AFIH.,

22.THIRUVARUR

Thyagaraja Temple
Address: Sannathi Street, Thiruvarur, Tamil Nadu 610001

Arulmigu Abathsahyeswarar Temple
Address: Sivan S St, Alangudi, Tamil Nadu 612801

Koothanur Maha Saraswathi Temple
Address: Kumbakonam Main Road, Koothanur, Tamil Nadu 609503

Sri Murugan Temple
Address: Engan, Tamil Nadu 610104

TAMILNADU REPORTER

Rajagopalaswamy Temple
Mannargudi

Varatharajan Pettai Maha Mariamman
Valangiman
Thuruvarur

Muthupet Lagoon
southern end of the Cauvery River, Thiruvarur
614704

Udayamarthandapuram Birds Sanctuary
Address: Pinnathur, Tamil Nadu 614706

Vaduvoor Bird Sanctuary
Address: Vaduvur Vadapthi, Tamil Nadu
614019

Dr. K.MURUGESAN , MBBS,AFIH.,

23.PUDUKKOTTAI

Periyanayagi Matha Church
Avoor,
Pudukkottai

Kunnandarkoil Cave Temple
Kunnandarkoil
Pudukottai

Thirupunavasal Vruddhapureeswarar Temple
Address: Thiruppunavasal, Tamil Nadu 614629

Kattubhava Pallivasal
10 km from Tirumaiyam
Pudukkottai

TAMILNADU REPORTER

Kudumiyanmalai
Annavasal
Pudukkottai

Viralimalai Murugan temple
Address: Neathaji Nagar, Viralimalai, Tamil
Nadu 621316

Sittanavasal Cave Temple
Address: Sittannavasal Cave Road,
Madiyanallur, Tamil Nadu 622101

Government Museum
Kalayanpuram, Pudukkottai 622005

Dr. K.MURUGESAN , MBBS,AFIH.,

24.DINDIGUL

Soundararajaperumal temple
Address: Dindigul District, Thadikombu, Tamil Nadu 624709

Palani Murugan temple
Address: Giri Veethi, Palani, Tamil Nadu 624601

Silver Cascade Falls
Address: Kodaikanal Ghat Road, Kodaikanal, Tamil Nadu 624101

Arulmigu Kottai Mariamman Temple
Address: Begambur, Dindigul, Tamil Nadu

TAMILNADU REPORTER

624001

Sirumalai Reserved Forests
Address: Sirumalai, Tamil Nadu 624003

Sri Abirami Amman Temple
Address: Chennai - Teni Hwy, Begambur,
Dindigul, Tamil Nadu 624001

Dindigul Fort
Address: Dindigul Fort Temple,
Muthalagupatty, Dindigul, Tamil Nadu 624001

Sri Chendraya Perumal Temple
Kottaipatti, Old Batlagundu
Dindigul
Tamil Nadu 624202

Bryant Park
Address: Lower Shola Rd, Kodaikanal, Tamil
Nadu 624101

Kodaikanal Solar Observatory
Address: Near Govt Rose Garden, Observatory

Dr. K.MURUGESAN , MBBS,AFIH.,

Rd, Kodaikanal, Tamil Nadu 624103

Kurinji Andavar Temple
Kurinji Andavar Temple Road
Kodaikanal, Tamil Nadu 624101

Sacred Heart College Museum
Address: Law's Ghat Road, Shenbaganur,
Kodaikanal, Tamil Nadu 624104

Saleth Matha Church
Address: Kodaikanal, Tamil Nadu 624101

Palani Murugan temple
Address: Giri Veethi, Palani, Tamil Nadu
624601

Kukkal Caves
Kukkal, Kodaikanal

25. SIVAGANGAI

Arulmigu Thiru Karpaga Vinayagar Temple
Address: Koothadipatti, Pillayarpatti, Tamil Nadu 630207

Shanmughanathar Temple
Address: Kundrakudi, Tamil Nadu 623305

Shri Amman Temple
Address: kallukatti, Karaikudi, Tamil Nadu 630001

Kaleeswarar koil
Address: Kalayarkoil, Tamil Nadu 630551

Dr. K.MURUGESAN , MBBS,AFIH.,

Vettangudi Bird Sanctuary
Address: Tirupattur,Sivagangai

Sree Muthumariamman Temple
Address: South Car Street, Thayamangalam,
Tamil Nadu 630709

Kodunkundreeswar Temple
Piranmalai
Tiruppathur Taluk
Sivagangai

Sri Tiruthali Nathar Temple
Tiruputhur-630 211,
Sivagangai

26.MADURAI

Meenakshi Amman Temple
Address: Madurai Main, Madurai, Tamil Nadu
625001

Thirumalai Nayakar Mahal
Madurai

Kallazhagar temple
Alagar Koyil
Madurai

Koodal Azhagar Temple
Address: Near Periyar Bus Stand, Madurai,
Tamil Nadu 625001

Dr. K.MURUGESAN , MBBS,AFIH.,

Gandhi Memorial Museum
Address: Tamukkam Park Road, Gandhi Nagar,
Near Collectorate, Madurai, Tamil Nadu
625020

Rajaji Park
Address: Alwarpuram, Madurai, Tamil Nadu
625020

Vandiyur Mariamman Teppakulam
Meenakshi Nagar, Madurai, Tamil Nadu
625009

27.THENI

Vaigai Dam
Address: Guest House Rd, Melmangalam,
Tamil Nadu 625562

Moongilanai Kamatchi Amman Temple
Address: Manjalar Dam Road, Devathana Patti,
Tamil Nadu 625602

Kumbakkarai Falls
Address: Kumbakarai Road,Periyakulam, Tamil
Nadu 624101

Dr. K.MURUGESAN , MBBS,AFIH.,

Theertha Thotti
Address: Periyakulam, Tamil Nadu 625601

Suruli Falls
Address: Near Cumbum, Suruli R.F., Tamil Nadu 625516

Kailasanathar Temple
Address: Dindigul - Theni - Kottarakkara Hwy, T. Kallipatti, Periyakulam, Tamil Nadu 625605

28.RAMANATHAPURAM

Pamban Bridge
Address: Rameswaram, Pamban, Tamil Nadu
623519

Ramanathaswamy Temple
Address: Rameswaram, Tamil Nadu 623526

Dhanushkodi Beach
Rameswaram

Annai Indira Gandhi Road Bridge
Rameswaram

Dr. K.MURUGESAN , MBBS,AFIH.,

Adam's Bridge - Rama Setu
Between Pamban Island and Mannar Island, Rameswaram

Sri Panchmukhi Hanuman Mandir & Floating Stones
Address: Rameswaram, Tamil Nadu 623526

Navagraha temple
Address: Devipattinam, Tamil Nadu 623514

Vivekananda Memorial House
Address: Rameswaram-Dhanushkodi Rd, Rameswaram, Tamil Nadu 623526

Dr. A.P.J. Abdul Kalam National Memorial
Address: Pamban- Tharavai Thoppu Rd, Pamban, Tamil Nadu 623529

Arulmigu Ramanatha Swamy Temple
Address: GP Rd, Rameswaram, Tamil Nadu 623526

Dhanushkodi Old Church
Address: Dhanushkodi, Tamil Nadu 623526

29.VIRUDHUNAGAR

Parasakthi Mariamman Temple
Address: Sivagami Puram, Virudhunagar, Tamil Nadu 626001

Pilavakkal Dam
Virudhunagar

Ayyanar Falls
Rajapalayam
Virudhunagar

Mariamman Temple
Address: Sattur, Irukkankudi, Tamil Nadu 626202

Sathuragiri Sundhara Mahalingam Temple
Address: Saptur R.F., Tamil Nadu 625705

Dr. K.MURUGESAN , MBBS,AFIH.,

Vaidyanathar temple
Address: Rajapalayam Road, Madavarvallagam, Srivilliputhur, Tamil Nadu 626125

Tirumalai Srinivasa Perumal Temple
Address: Tiruvanamalai, Srivilliputtur TK, srivilliputtur, Virdhunagar Dist, Venkateswarapuram, Tamil Nadu 626125

Badrakali Amman temple
Address: Parasakthi Colony, Sivakasi, Tamil Nadu 626123

Award City Theme Park
Address: Virudhunagar - T Kalluppatty - Maravapatty Rd, Puliankulam, Tamil Nadu 625707

30.THOOTHUKUDI

Shankara Rameshwarar kovil
Address: 18, S Sambantha Moorthy St,
Tuticorin Melur, Shanmugapuram,
Thoothukudi, Tamil Nadu 628001

Roche Park
Address: Beach Road, Tuticorin Beach Road
Salt Pans, Thoothukudi, Tamil Nadu 628001

Church of Our Lady of Snows
Address: Plot No.41, Beach Road, Tuticorin,
Thoothukudi, Tamil Nadu 628001

Kalugumalai Murugan Temple
Address: Temple Tank, Kalugumalai, Tamil
Nadu 628552

Dr. K.MURUGESAN , MBBS,AFIH.,

Korkai Temple
Address:Korkai , Valavallan, Tamil Nadu 628801

Vallanadu Black Buck Sanctuary
Address: Vallanadu R.F., Tamil Nadu 628851

Sri Mariamman Temple
Address: Savalaperi-Deivaseyalpuram Rd, Deivacheyalpuram, Tamil Nadu 628851

Thiruchendur Murugan temple
Address: Tiruchendur, Tamil Nadu 628215

Veerapandiya Kattabomman Memorial Fort
Address: Panchalankurichi, Tamil Nadu 628401

31.THIRUNELVELI

Nellaiappar Temple
Address: 162, E Car St, Tirunelveli Town,
Tirunelveli, Tamil Nadu 627006

Arulmigu Sankaranarayanaswamy Temple
Address: Tirunelveli, Sankarankovil, Tamil
Nadu 627756

Courtallam Main Falls
Address: Courtallam, Tirunelveli, Tamil Nadu
627802

Papanasanathar temple
Upper Dam Rd, State Highway178, Tirunelveli
627425

Kalakkad Mundanthurai Tiger Reserve
Address: Ambasamudram - Papanasam -

Dr. K.MURUGESAN , MBBS,AFIH.,

Upper Dam Rd, Papanasam R.F., Tamil Nadu
627551

Kalakkadu Sanctuary
Near Western Ghats,
Tirunelveli

Koothankulam Bird Sanctuary
Kunthankulam
Nanguneri Taluk
Tirunelveli

Ariyakulam Bird Sanctuary
Tirunelveli

Athankarai Pallivasal
Address: Radhapuram - Ramankudi Rd,
Athankarai, Pallivasal, Tamil Nadu 627111

Kasi Viswanathar Kovil
Address: Tenkasi, Tamil Nadu 627811

32.KANYA KUMARI

Arulmigu Bhagavathy Amman Temple
Address: Temple Road, Kanyakumari, Tamil Nadu 629702

Kamarajar Memorial
Address: Kanyakumari, Tamil Nadu 629702

Government Museum
Address: Beach Rd, Kanyakumari, Tamil Nadu 629702

Guganatheeswarar Temple
Address: Kanyakumari, Tamil Nadu 629702

Vattakottai Fort
Address: Vattakkottai, Tamil Nadu 629401

Dr. K.MURUGESAN , MBBS,AFIH.,

Thanumalayan Temple
Address: N Car St, Vivekananda Junction,
Suchindram, Tamil Nadu 629704

Udayagiri Fort
Puliyoorkurichi,
Thiruvananthapuram-Nagercoil National
Highway, Kanyakumari

Padmanabhapuram Palace
Padmanabhapuram, Kalkulam taluk,
Kanyakumari

Pechiparai Reservoir
Pechiparai , Kanyakumari

Mandaikadu Bhagavathi Amman Temple
Address: SH 46, Mandaikadu, Tamil Nadu
629252

TAMILNADU REPORTER

Dr. K.MURUGESAN , MBBS,AFIH.,

ABOUT THE AUTHOR

My name is Dr . K .Murugesan . I am A doctor . I have completed MBBS and AFIH . Contact me to give updates on tourist places in Tamilnadu which will be published in the next edition .my mail id is : doctor_india@hotmail.com

TAMILNADU REPORTER

DISCLAIMER :
The information provided within this book is for general informational purposes only. While we try to keep the information up-to-date and correct, there are no representations or warranties, express or implied, about the completeness, accuracy, reliability, suitability or availability with respect to the information, products, services, or related graphics contained in this book for any purpose. Any use of this information is at your own risk.